Materials

1 allergy-free metal: ε

For people with metal allerg... ...ings can present
great difficulty. Now earwire ...ole in a variety of colors in
niobium, a natural element that is 100% irritation-free. I have a
severe metal allergy, and this year I discovered niobium. It truly
is non-allergenic. What a joy it is to wear earrings again.
– *Jamie Lesser, Milwaukee, Wis.*

2 seed bead best bets

Japanese cylinder beads are uniform in size and are perfect for
patterns where seed bead count requires precise measurement.
Czech seed beads are irregular in size and are great for creating
texture. – *Cassie McGuinn, Austin, Texas*

3 elastic ribbon

Use a multi-filament ribbon elastic instead of mono-filament
elastic for stringing projects involving more expensive beads.
If multi-filament elastic catches a sharp bead or edge, it will fray
before it breaks, giving you a chance to rescue the piece. Mono-
filament elastic is less expensive, but it breaks more easily.
– *Ann Bergermann, Orlando, Fla.*

4 wirework

Soft wire strengthens when hammered, but any wire will become
brittle and susceptible to breakage if overworked. Work wire as
little as possible. – *M. Lovell, Toledo, Ohio*

5 the key to shopping

When I have some beads for a project, but need additional
components, I string the beads on a head pin, make a wrapped
loop, and attach the loop to my keychain. The keychain keeps
the beads accessible so that I can shop for the rest of the
materials whenever I am out. – *Linda Stark, Jacksonville, Fla.*

Inspiration

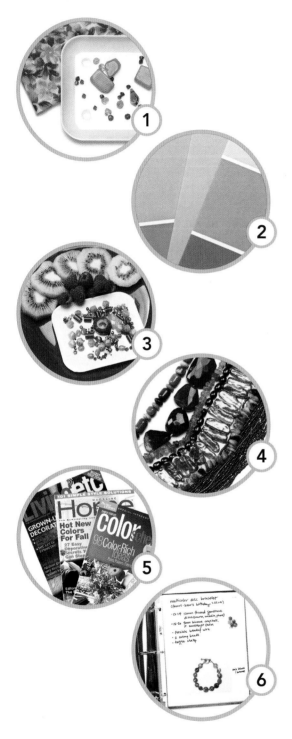

1 fabric inspiration

Are you unsure of how to select colors for your jewelry designs? Go to your local fabric store and look at printed fabrics until one catches your eye. Buy a small piece and study the colors. Then, match beads to the colors and work them into a jewelry design. This approach will work even if you like monochromatic color schemes because you'll see the range of colors used to achieve that effect. – *Beth Stone, via e-mail*

2 paint chips

When I'm considering colors for a project, I go to the hardware store and select an assortment of paint chips. Since they are portable, reusable, and easy to sort, chips help me see a variety of possible colors and design arrangements. – *Charlee Cole, Los Angeles, Calif.*

3 good taste

Food and cooking magazines feature seasonal ideas and interesting combinations of colors and textures. I find them as inspirational as fashion magazines for jewelry design ideas. – *C. Francis, via e-mail*

4 swap meet

My friends and I get together not only to make jewelry, but also to swap beads and ideas. Spending time with one another helps stir our creative juices and encourages new possibilities for old beads. Plus, one person's trash truly can be another person's treasure. – *T. Duncan, via e-mail*

5 home sweet home

Home decorating magazines are a great source of jewelry-design inspiration since they present patterns, textures, and colors in unexpected ways. – *M. Rae Smith, Wauwatosa, Wis.*

6 project scrapbook

Keep track of your projects in a beading scrapbook. On a sheet of paper, write down a materials list. In the top corner, staple a few leftover beads in a small, resealable bag. Then, tape a photo of the finished piece to the bottom of the page. Add project notes (such as the cost or helpful tips). Finally, insert the page into a sheet protector, and file it in a three-ring binder. – *Erika Barrientes, Brownsville, Texas*

7 vintage variety

Buy vintage chains at thrift stores or rummage sales. You'll find some great deals as well as a variety of colors and finishes not otherwise available. Mix and match old and new chains to create a fantastic new piece. – *T. Sebastian, via e-mail*

8 breaking news: on-air style

Watch TV news to catch inspiration from the anchorwomen's necklaces – most of them wear eye-catching jewelry. Many female TV journalists are beading their own jewelry these days. While you watch, sketch design ideas and make notes on bead size, color, spacing, drape, and length. – *Karin Buckingham, Oconomowoc, Wis.*

9 natural wonders

Go for a walk outdoors and capture the colors and shapes that appear together in nature. Sketch or photograph your favorite flowers or trees. Photograph sunsets, paint the blue-green shades of a lake, or copy the patterns from a rock formation. Keep these images in a folder you take to the bead store, so you can match bead colors, shapes, and textures with your impressions of nature. – *Rachelle Unger, Phoenix, Ariz.*

10 window shopping

Always check the display windows of your favorite shops when you're out walking in town. Jewelry stores, of course, will have expensive versions of what you can make at home for a fraction of the cost. Many clothing and accessories stores display hand-made jewelry along with the latest fashions. Make a mental note of what you like. When you get home, sketch a design and jot down color possibilities. – *Melvina St. James, Palo Alto, Calif.*

11 tired of trends?

Go to your public library and peruse archived periodicals such as *Vogue*. Keep an eye out for interesting color, form, and texture worn by the models and update the look with today's materials. – *Haley Wilcox, Middletown, Conn.*

12 second-chance clasps

Visit flea markets or tag sales that offer second-hand costume jewelry. Surprisingly, even damaged or otherwise unappealing pieces can sometimes include interesting clasps. Separate these vintage clasps and give them new life as the centerpiece of a new project. – *Marie Schalk, Alexander, Ark.*

Sorting & handling

1 sorting beads

To sort beads of various sizes, position a colander over a large bowl and pour the beads into it. The smallest beads will fall through the colander's holes. This method works especially well to separate seed beads from larger beads. – *Judy Danielson, Marble Falls, Texas*

2 checking colorfastness

To determine if gemstone beads have been dyed, dip them in warm water. If the water changes color, the beads have been dyed. You also can clean gemstones with warm water. Just add a little mild dishwashing liquid and rinse. – *N. Hunter, via e-mail*

3 totally tubular

Keep your empty seed bead tubes for scooping up beads when it's clean-up time. Tuck a small clear tube near your beading board, and it'll be ready at hand when you're moving, sorting, or scooping quantities of beads. – *Melissa Watkins, Ann Arbor, Mich.*

4 clamshell shovel

I make jewelry on a padded board. After I'm done with a project, I use a clamshell to gather any stray beads. It's easy to shovel up beads by pressing the shell lightly into the board, and the shell's curved shape and narrow edge make quick work of pouring tiny beads back into tubes. – *Lauren Procarione, Greenfield, Wis.*

5 paper-cup pouring

Roll beads from your work surface into a small paper cup, flatten it, and pour the beads into their storage container. This low-cost solution is efficient and prevents beads from spilling. – *Nancy McKee, San Ysidro, Calif.*

6 home plate

I use inexpensive paper plates as bead trays because their fluted edges keep beads from rolling away. When finished, I simply bend the plate in half and pour the beads into a container. The plates also work well as rests for open glue tubes, keeping the stickiness away from my work surface. – *Diane Underwood, via e-mail*

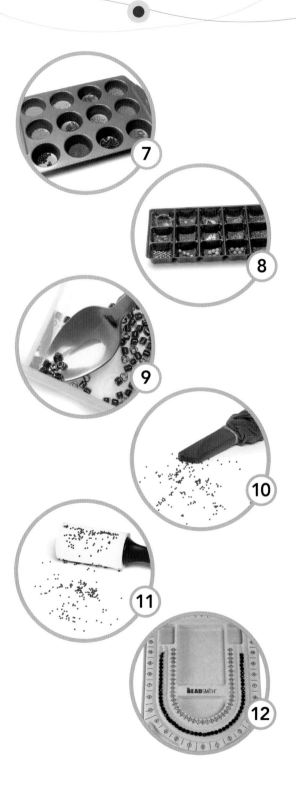

7 muffin tins

Use a muffin tin to sort beads. With a dozen cups, a tin is perfect for projects that require many different beads. To make cleanup easier, put paper liners in the tins first, then simply pour the beads back into their containers. – *C. C. Lilly, via e-mail*

8 box of chocolates

After you finish that Valentine's Day box of chocolates, clean the plastic tray and use it to sort beads. The tray holds small quantities of many kinds of beads and findings, which is helpful when stringing a complicated piece. – *Samantha Bond, via e-mail*

9 spoon scoops

A souvenir or baby spoon makes a great scoop for tiny beads. It can get into the corners of a tray or design board for easy bead pick up. With a slightly pointed tip, the spoon is also handy for putting beads back in small containers or tubes. – *Shawn Szilvasi, via e-mail*

10 don't cry over spills

Stretch a knee-high stocking over your vacuum cleaner hose and then vacuum up spilled seed beads. The suction will hold the seed beads in the nylon stocking until you are ready to brush the beads back to safety on your worktable. – *Jean Rufus, Kansas City, Mo.*

11 quick pick up

Use an adhesive lint roller to pick up spilled beads. – *Vivian L. Hiller, Milwaukee, Wis.*

12 stay in the groove

Place a strand of gemstones in the groove of your beading board before removing the string. This will keep the beads in a graduated order. – *Beatrice Jaimes, Dallas, Texas*

Organization & storage

1 seed bead reminders
When working with seed beads, it's difficult to remember the names and item numbers of each color. Simplify the task by making labels with the beads' color, style number, and source. You'll save time by not having to sort through many similar colors in a store or catalog. – *Jasmine Michaels, via e-mail*

2 not just for babies
Although glass baby food jars have long been used as storage containers, the new plastic ones with snap-on tops are also a great option. They are clear, stackable, easy to carry, and best of all, unbreakable. – *Mary Marzano, Delray Beach, Fla.*

3 labeling wire
Store wire in a plastic, zip-top bag to see its gauge at a glance. Attach a piece of transparent tape to the bag and label the wire gauge, type, and hardness. It's easy to remove the tape and recycle the bag once the wire has been used. – *Grace Carter, Denver, Colo.*

4 scrap storage
Keep empty beading-wire spools to store cut pieces of beading wire. The spool helps the wire retain its shape and stay kink-free.
– *Christie Nagata, Hilo, Hawaii*

5 wire at a glance
I like to organize spools of flexible beading wire in stacks, but want to know their sizes without removing each spool. The solution: Label each spool's plastic cuff with the wire's diameter. Use a permanent marker. Affix a small white sticker to black or clear plastic. You'll see each wire's thickness immediately.
– *R. Podell, Milwaukee, Wis.*

6 utensil trays
Use a wooden or plastic utensil tray to organize materials and projects. The compartments are the ideal size for storing beads, findings, and tools; longer sections work well for bead strands or unfinished projects. Sturdy and portable, the tray will help you see project options at a glance. – *C. Atkins, via e-mail*

7 carried away
For upright and portable organization, store your seed beads in a picnic or restaurant-style utensil carrier. Each compartment holds 15 or more tubes, so you can keep 90–100 tubes within reach. Plus, the carrier keeps the tubes upright – helpful if you work with several different colors at one time. – *H. C. Mercer, via e-mail*

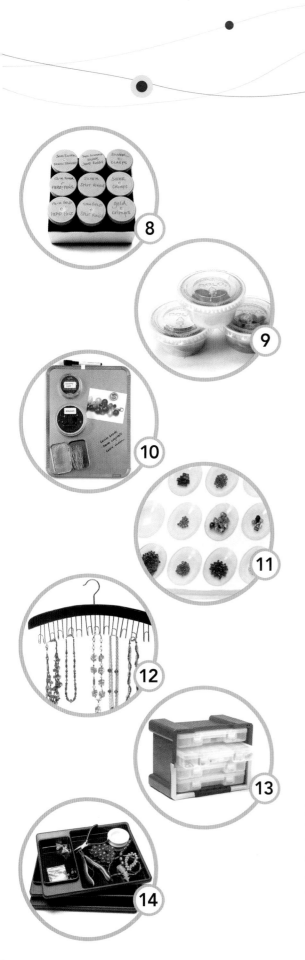

8 smart storage

Store tiny essentials, such as crimp beads and jump rings, in 35mm-film canisters. With a permanent marker, label each canister with its contents. To make findings more accessible, arrange the canisters you use most in the front of a tray or box. – *Veronica Miller, Pittsburgh, Pa.*

9 storage on the go

For secure, visible storage, stack beads and findings in plastic cups with clear covers. Save the containers from restaurant take-out, or purchase them in bulk from a discount store. For added convenience, organize the cups on a revolving tray. – *Susan Van Voorhees, Columbia, Md.*

10 magnetic personality

Organize findings in metal tins that previously held mints or candles. Attach self-adhesive magnetic tape to the tins and place them on a magnetic bulletin board. (You can find magnetic tape and bulletin boards at office-supply stores.) You also can display lists or photos of design ideas. – *Laura Georgy, Quincy, Mass.*

11 deviled-egg tray

Use an oyster plate or deviled-egg tray to separate beads by color and type when working on a project. Egg trays have many sections, and their depth makes them especially well-suited to organizing seed beads or small crystals and gemstones. – *Lynne Sheldon, Deerfield, Ill.*

12 jewelry hang ups

A belt hanger with hooks is a handy way to store jewelry. The holder organizes twelve or more necklaces while occupying minimal space in your closet, and jewelry is less likely to get tangled or tarnished. – *E. Jones, via e-mail*

13 tidy tote

Pick up a plastic organizer from your local home-improvement store. This one has four drawers with multiple compartments, a handle that folds down, and holes for wall mounting – all for only $10. – *Ruth Zamarripa, Los Gatos, Calif.*

14 double-duty trays

Playing with bead combinations for a while before committing to one design is a practice of mine, but sometimes I lose pieces when working on multiple projects. Now I keep the pieces of each project together in recycled frozen dinner trays. The trays have high walls and can be stacked – a benefit if you work on several projects simultaneously or have limited work space. (You can also use airline-food trays, available at surplus stores.) – *Brenda Schweder, via e-mail*

Tools

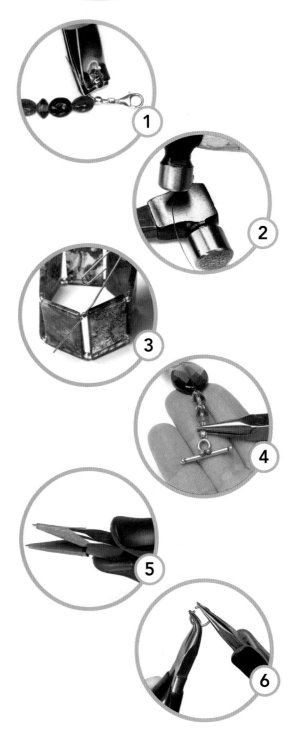

1 clip it

When working on a wire or stringing project, a pair of nail clippers is handy for making quick, close cuts. Clippers also relieve hand strain; you can trim with one hand, rather than hold a set of wire cutters with one hand and pull the wire taut with the other. – *Julia Prater, via e-mail*

2 hammer time

Hardening head pins or findings usually requires a bench block or anvil. In a pinch, substitute a large hammer turned on its side. The hammer's head provides a hard, flat surface for pounding the wire. – *Pam Pollard, Coweta, Okla.*

3 unconventional tool

As silly as it sounds, I find that an unbent paper clip works wonders when you need a small, pointed tool. I use the clip to push knots into beads, move errant beads away from a bail, and straighten necklaces on displays. – *Lisa Jefferson, via e-mail*

4 chainnose tip

Use the tip of your chainnose pliers rather than crimping pliers to crimp between two seed beads. It is easier to see the seed beads and, therefore, avoid crushing them. – *Ruthanne Davis, Colorado Springs, Colo.*

5 gentler pliers

Cover the jaws of your chainnose pliers with painter's tape to prevent the pliers from marring your wire or component. Unlike transparent tape, painter's tape has a little bit of grip to its surface and is easy to remove. – *M. T. Banks, via e-mail*

6 bentnose grip

Although bentnose pliers aren't required for most jewelry projects, they're indispensable for opening and closing jump rings. They'll give you a secure grip and are less likely to mar the surface. – *M. J. Rose, via e-mail*

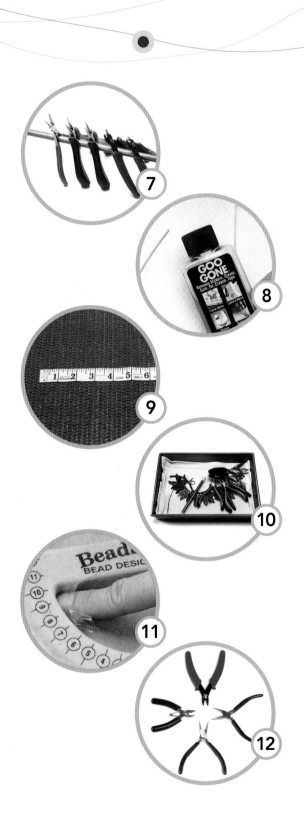

7 tool bar

Using an inexpensive towel bar keeps your beading tools organized and easily accessible. Buy one with substantial wall mounts, prop it up on your work space, and place the tools over the bar. – *Marissa McConnell, via e-mail*

8 squeaky clean

Sterling or gold-filled wire is often sold in coils, taped together. To remove tape residue, use an adhesive remover such as Goo Gone. Simply moisten a rag and rub it on the wire for low-effort cleaning. – *Veronica Stewart, via e-mail*

9 space that measures up

I designed my own inexpensive beading surface using textured-foam shelf liner and a cloth tape measure. Cut approximately 28 in. (71cm) of liner and staple a 24-in. (61cm) length of tape measure across the bottom. The liner is inexpensive and portable, beads won't roll off the surface, and you'll always know the length of your work-in-progress. – *Martha Wilderman, St. Peters, Mo.*

10 beading tray

A metal cookie sheet or large baking pan can double as a portable tray to hold your projects and tools. Simply line the pan with a dish towel, and your loose beads and findings will stay put. When you're done with a project, shake out the towel over a waste basket to prevent wire clippings and broken beads from becoming embedded in your work space. – *Jane Posten-Buckley, New York, N.Y.*

11 clean across the board

Dust, broken beads, and tiny pieces of wire often get stuck in the channels of a bead-design board. To clean the board, use a piece of mailing or packing tape. Just push the tape into the channels and corners to remove the dust. Your board will look brand new! – *Cheryl Cassidy, Springfield, Mass.*

12 cool tool arrangement

It may not be brain surgery, but why not organize your tools like a surgeon does? Keeping your tools in order on your work table can save you time and distraction. Arrange your tools in a progressive pattern, such as by size or frequency of use. Or, model your setup after a mental image such as tree branches, a clock face, or a ladder. Train your mind and memory to reach for the tool you need without looking. Remember to put the tool back in the same place every time. – *Martha Driver, Chicago, Ill.*

Technique

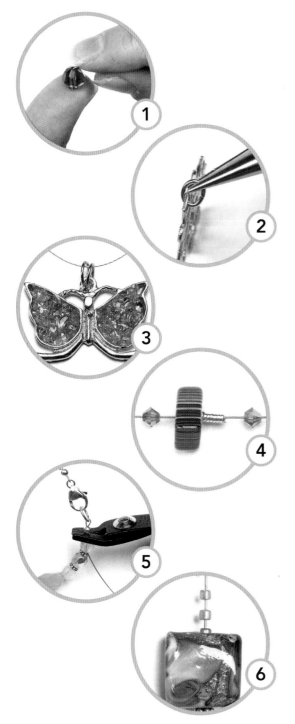

1 plain-loop perfection
To make plain loops, put your finger against the head pin, underneath the bead. You'll be able to bend the head pin closer to the bead, so your loop will show less excess wire. – *Sarah Keefe, Boston, Mass.*

2 oval jump rings
For extra security when a project calls for unsoldered jump rings, substitute oval jump rings: A clasp, pendant, or charm will hang safely away from the jump ring's opening, making it less likely to detach accidentally. – *Sandra Porter, via e-mail*

3 secure jump rings
If you like the security of split rings but prefer the look of jump rings, use two jump rings as a compromise. You can substitute double jump rings when making a bail (shown) or when linking charms or dangles to chain. – *Y. Funatsu, via e-mail*

4 furnace-glass bead solution
When stringing a large-hole furnace-glass bead, string a wire coil to nestle inside the bead's hole. Make coils by wrapping 24-gauge wire around an 18- or 20-gauge wire. Remove the coiled wire and cut it to fit within the bead. The coils prevent smaller beads from becoming lodged inside the furnace-glass bead. – *Veronica Stewart, via e-mail*

5 careful crimping
When finishing a strung bracelet with a lobster claw clasp and a soldered jump ring, crimp the clasp end first. Fasten the clasp to the jump ring before crimping the other end. This will keep the jump ring away from the crimp bead. Finishing while the piece is in a curved shape will also ensure that the bracelet is not crimped too tightly. – *R. Diamond, via e-mail*

6 seed bead bail-out
To make a bail for a large-hole bead, string size 8º or 10º seed beads on a head pin to fit inside the larger bead. The seed beads will prevent the head pin from moving around and will help the large bead hang evenly. – *Anne Peterson, via e-mail*

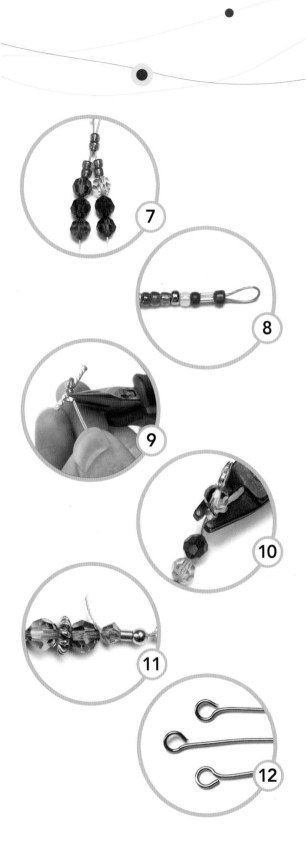

7 two-strand solution

To string two strands of beading wire through a bead with a small hole, cut one wire slightly shorter than the other. You'll find it easier to string one wire at a time through a bead.
– *Laurie James, New York, N.Y.*

8 loops with beading wire

I often finish seed bead necklaces with beading-wire loops so I can slide art beads or pendants on and off easily. String a crimp bead and a seed bead, go back through the beads leaving a loop, and make a folded crimp. The wire loop substitutes for a jump ring or split ring. Use a lobster claw clasp to finish the other end.
– *Lynne Dixon-Speller, Wauwatosa, Wis.*

9 crimping compromise

For foolproof crimping, I use both crimping and chainnose pliers. First, I use the lower grooves in the crimping pliers to create the fold in the crimp bead. Then, I use chainnose pliers to fold the crimp in half. This method creates a secure crimp with less likelihood of breaking adjacent beads. – *M. R. Miller, Evanston, Ill.*

10 removing flattened crimps

When you need to remove a flattened crimp bead, crimping pliers work far better than chainnose pliers, which tend to slip. Position the notch closest to the tip around the crimp and squeeze gently. The crimp bead will become round and will slide easily off the wire. – *Elizabeth Ferris, Carrboro, N.C.*

11 cutting at an angle

During a stringing project, the ends of flexible beading wire can fray. To make finishing a breeze, trim the wire's end at an angle; the narrow tip will go back through beads more easily.
– *J. Warner, via e-mail*

12 quick eye pins

To make eye pins, trim the head from a head pin and make a plain loop at one end, or make a plain loop on the end of a 2-in. (5cm) piece of 22-gauge wire. – *N. St. George, Miami, Fla.*

Technique

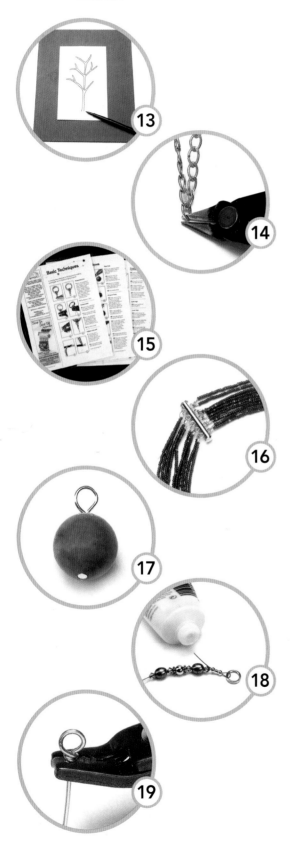

13 branch out with wire
Create wire patterns easily by drawing them first. To mimic the way you will work with wire, do the following: Put the tip of your pencil on a piece of paper. Without lifting the pencil, draw a shape – without crossing any lines. The drawing will give you an idea of what pattern to follow and where to bend the wire.
– *Pat Ritter, via e-mail*

14 cutting chain
To get two even pieces of chain from one longer one, fold the chain in half and string each of the end links on a head pin. You'll have either one or two links hanging at the bottom. If you have one link, cut it. If you have two, cut both. You'll be left with equal lengths, without having to count the links.
– *Taryn Yager-Sayles, Roseville, Minn.*

15 convenient reference
I removed the Basic Techniques section of *BeadStyle* and laminated each page at a copy store. I put the sheets on my bulletin board or in my bead box for easy reference. That way, there's no need to flip pages back and forth as I work on a project in the magazine. – *B. Earl, Denver, Colo.*

16 a graceful drape
Before crimping, check the fit of a necklace while it's in a circular position (as it would be worn). This will ensure flexibility and a graceful drape to the necklace after finishing. – *Suzanne Gold, Los Angeles, Calif.*

17 practice makes perfect
Practice making wire loops using inexpensive head pins until you are satisfied with your technique. Or buy a spool of copper wire from a hardware or craft store and practice making loops with that. – *Julie Rushmore, Atlanta, Ga.*

18 smooth finish
When finishing a strung necklace or bracelet, dab the end of the flexible beading wire with hand lotion. The wire will go back through the beads more easily. – *Laura Bub, East Granby, Conn.*

19 snip and tuck
To tuck wire wraps close to the stem of a wrapped loop, use the round notch of your crimping pliers. Position the notch closest to the tip around the trimmed end of the wraps and squeeze gently. You'll have a neat finish without flattening the wraps. – *S. Foster, Newton, Mass.*

Clasps & extensions

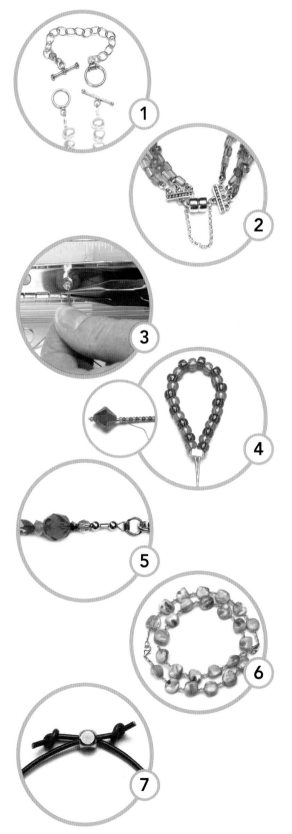

1 toggle extenders
It's easy to extend the length of a necklace that has a toggle clasp. Attach each end of a 3-in. (7.6cm) chain to each half of a second toggle clasp. To wear, insert the extender's bar end into the necklace's loop end and vice versa. – *Ruth Wallace, via e-mail*

2 keeping it together
Magnetic clasps are easier to fasten than other types of clasps, particularly on bracelets. To make a closure more secure, attach a short piece (about 2 in./5cm) of chain to the clasp's loops with jump rings. With the safety chain, there is less risk of losing the bracelet if the clasp opens. – *Patricia Russo, Medina, Ohio*

3 magnetic clasp reminder
When planning to finish a necklace or bracelet with a magnetic clasp, remember that your tools may snap onto the clasp, making it difficult to work. Solution: Attach the magnet clasp to a metal ruler or a large metal surface, like a refrigerator, while using tools for finishing. – *Cheryl Grosjean, via e-mail*

4 out of clasps? make your own.
Make your own clasp out of a large bead or button and a loop of seed beads. String a crimp bead, large bead, and a seed bead at one end. Skip the seed bead and go back through the large bead and the crimp bead. Crimp. On the other end, string a crimp bead and enough seed beads to fit over the large bead. Go back through the crimp bead and crimp. – *Karin Buckingham, Oconomowoc, Wis.*

5 flexible finishing
To build flexibility into a strung bracelet's length, string a crimp bead and spacer on the end of the bracelet. String another crimp bead onto a jump ring. Thread the wire through the jump ring's crimp bead, go back through the last beads strung, and crimp the bracelet's crimp bead. Attach the clasp with a jump ring. You can adjust the length by adding extra jump rings to the first one, without restringing the bracelet. – *Marie Rankin, via e-mail*

6 necklace extenders
A bracelet is a handy extender for a necklace; simply finish both pieces with lobster claw clasps and soldered jump rings. To wear, attach the bracelet's clasp to the necklace's jump ring and vice versa. Wear the new length as a long necklace, or wrap it twice for a choker or three times for a chunky bracelet. – *B. Davis, via e-mail*

7 tying up loose ends
It's easy to make an adjustable closure for a leather necklace. First, make sure your cord is long enough to slip over your head. Next, string the ends through a large-hole bead in opposite directions and tie an overhand knot at each end. Put the necklace on, and pull the ends to adjust its length. – *Peggy Thomas, Ridgefield, Conn.*

Tricks

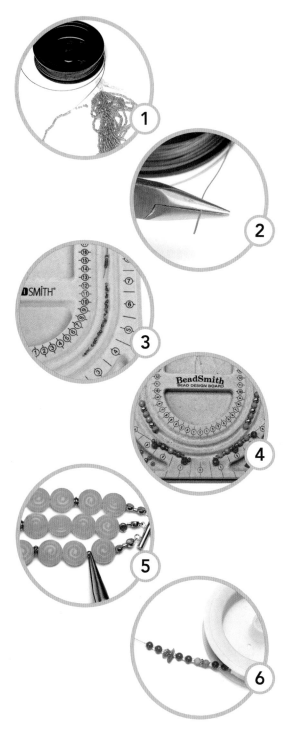

1 for faster stringing

For faster stringing, transfer seed beads directly from the hank to the flexible beading wire. – *T. Rotide, Waukesha, Wis.*

2 easier threading

If you find certain beads difficult to thread, flatten the tip of your beading wire with chainnose pliers first. – *S. Alexander, San Diego, Calif.*

3 quick beading

For quick beading, line up separate rows of seed beads in the channels of a bead-design board. Slide the tip of your beading wire through the whole row at once, rather than stringing one bead at a time. – *E. Alvarez, Albuquerque, N.M.*

4 head pin arrangements

When designing a piece of jewelry, string combinations of beads and spacers on long head pins. Rearrange the head pins on a bead-design board to see how the combinations look together. You will save time when stringing different patterns and reorganizing groups of beads. – *Marie Rankin, via e-mail*

5 bridging the gap

If you see a gap between beads in a finished piece, fill the space with a crimp cover. Select a silver- or gold-colored crimp cover to match your design, then simply close the cover over the beading wire – no restringing required. – *Elizabeth Wall, Irvington, N.J.*

6 spooling around

To simplify a stringing project, unroll a length of beading wire slightly longer than what you'll need. Put the plastic spool cover back on and begin stringing. Don't cut the wire until you're ready to add the clasp. Stringing onto the spool reduces the amount of excess wire you use, while keeping the nonworking end of the wire secure. – *Gigi Burgess, Milwaukee, Wis.*

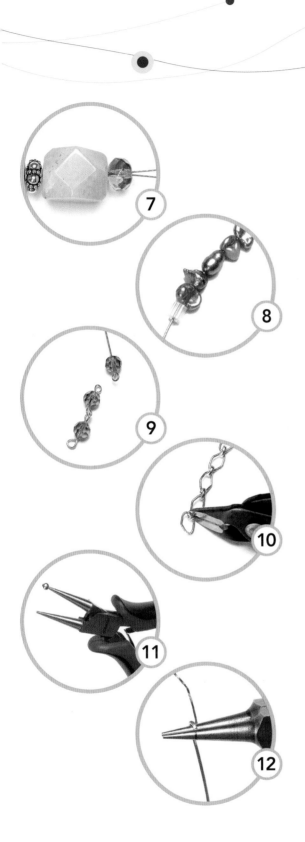

7 sturdy strands

Instead of using a large-diameter flexible beading wire to string heavy beads, I use two strands of .014 or .015 wire. If one strand breaks, the second provides reinforcement and holds the beads together. Just make sure the beads at the ends of the piece have holes large enough to accommodate four strands of wire.
– *Dee Martin, via e-mail*

8 earring backups

Instead of using tape to secure the ends of beading wire while you work, use rubber earring backs. They are easy to remove and reposition, and they don't leave a sticky residue on your wire.
– *Lisa LeClaire-Taylor, New York, N.Y.*

9 missing links

If you do a project requiring many beaded links, consider using purchased eye pins. You'll save yourself a lot of work. – *Yoshi Harper, Los Angeles, Calif.*

10 jump rings in a pinch

If you are finishing a piece of jewelry and realize that you need a soldered jump ring, you can substitute a link of chain. Simply cut the next-to-last link of chain and use the last link in place of a soldered jump ring. – *B. Wells, via e-mail*

11 enlarging a bead hole

If the hole of a metal bead is too small for multiple strands of wire to pass through, place the bead on the tip of one jaw of your roundnose pliers. Twist the pliers gently a couple times to enlarge the hole. – *May Frank, via e-mail*

12 consistent loops

With a permanent marker, indicate on the jaws of your roundnose pliers where you wrap wire loops. Use the mark as a guide to make the size of plain or wrapped loops consistent. If necessary, remove the mark with rubbing alcohol. – *R. Davis, Cleveland, Ohio*

Presentation

1 package deals

Many bead catalogs carry packaging and display items, such as jewelry boxes, gift bags, tissue paper, and ribbons for purchase in bulk. Even if you don't sell your jewelry, it's convenient to have packages on hand if you give your jewelry as gifts. To reduce the cost, share an order with a friend. – *T. B. Scott, via e-mail*

2 revolving display

To display many earrings, hang them in the holes of an inverted mesh trash can. Place the trash can on a lazy Susan, and spin the lazy Susan to see your jewelry at a glance. – *Catie Hoover, via e-mail*

3 earring display

To make an inexpensive earring holder, attach a piece of needlepoint canvas to the clips on a skirt hanger. Hook earrings through the holes in the canvas, and hang the holder in a closet for convenient storage. You'll be able to see all your earrings at a glance. – *Cindy Klein, Tucson, Ariz.*

4 pitcher perfect

For a pretty, functional jewelry display, hang earrings on the rim of a pitcher, mug, bowl, or vase. (The larger the rim, the more pairs you can hang.) The inside of the container can hold earrings that need repair or have lost their mates. – *Amanda Bohm, Austin, Texas*

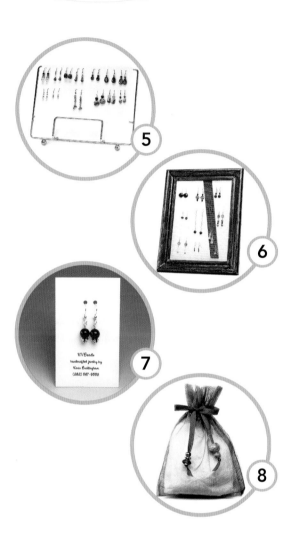

5 earring board

Buy a cookbook stand at any kitchen supply store, hardware store, or discount chain. Take a piece of smooth white cardboard (men's shirts, new or starched from the cleaners, are packaged with these). Prop the piece of white cardboard up on the bookstand. Poke rows of pairs of tiny holes using the sharp point of a pushpin. Leave room vertically for dangle earrings to hang. Arrange your finished or in-process earrings across the board. This display board allows you to view a complete collection at once. You can evaluate your collection for variety and harmony before you add designs or make duplicates.
– *Greta Hauser, Pittsburgh, Pa.*

6 framed screening

Fit a piece of screen into a picture frame in place of the glass; hang earrings through the holes in the screen. – *A. Singer, New York, N.Y.*

7 earring cards

Make earring cards using your computer and clean-edge business card pages. Punch two holes in the card to hang the earrings. I use a two-hole punch from a scrapbook store to make even holes. A micro-hole puncher works as well.
– *Karin Buckingham, Oconomowoc, Wis.*

8 easy embellishment

Beaded ribbons make easy, pretty decorations for gift boxes or bags. Thread a few leftover beads on a piece of organza or satin ribbon and tie a knot at each end. When wrapping a large box, tie a ribbon around it first, then thread beads, knot the ends, and trim the excess ribbon. – *L.D. Fisher, Oakland, Calif.*

Get Great Jewelry Projects All Through the Year!

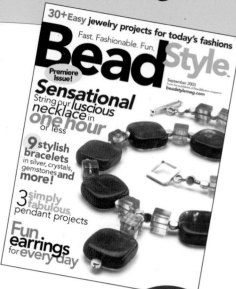

Your Beading Resource!

Bead&Button magazine

- New and traditional stitching techniques
- Fully-tested projects
- Step-by-step instructions and photos

BeadStyle magazine

- Beautiful pieces in today's hottest styles
- Make jewelry in an evening or less
- Great photos and easy-to-follow instructions

If you enjoyed *101 Best Beading Tips*, make sure you order these titles from the Easy-Does-It Series.

Subscribe or Order Today and Enjoy
New Beading Projects Every Month!
Call 1-800-533-6644 or visit
beadandbuttonbooks.com

KALMBACH PUBLISHING CO.

ISBN 978-0-89024-677-1

$7.95 U.S. 12337
$10.95 CAN

90000